MINIMUM HEROIC

ALSO BY CHRISTOPHER SALERNO

WHIRLIGIG (2006)

Minimum Heroic

Christopher Salerno

The Mississippi Review Poetry Series
Hattiesburg 2010

Published by the *Mississippi Review*, Hattiesburg, MS 39406

Copyright © 2010, Christopher Salerno

Manufactured in the United States of America

10 9 8 7 6 5 4 3 2 1

ISBN 978-0-9842652-2-0

ISSN 0047-7559

Mississippi Review Volume 37 Number 3 ~ Book 3 of 3

The author would like to thank the editors of the following journals in which some of these poems first appeared, occasionally in different versions: *Colorado Review*, *American Letters & Commentary*, *Free Verse*, *Denver Quarterly*, *Boston Review*, *Coconut*, *Octopus Magazine*, *MiPOesias*, *The Carolina Quarterly*, and *The Laurel Review*. Special thanks to The *Mississippi Review* Poetry Series and to Dara Wier for selecting this book. Thanks also to Tom Lisk, Emily Arnold, John Gallaher, Benjamin Paloff, Justin Marks, Chris Tonelli, and, of course, Jess.

Mississippi Review is published twice a year by the Center for Writers, The University of Southern Mississippi (AA/EOE/ADAI), 118 College Drive, #5144, Hattiesburg, MS 39406-0001. Editor: Frederick Barthelme. Managing Editor: Rie Fortenberry. Associate Editors: Angela Ball, Steven Barthelme, Julia Johnson. Assistant Editors: Lynn Watson, Elizabeth Wagner, Beth Couture. Subscription rates: $15 per year for individuals, $32 for institutions. Foreign subscriptions $10 per year additional. Single copies $9. *Mississippi Review* wishes to acknowledge the kind support of the National Endowment for the Arts. The views expressed herein are those of the authors, not the editors or sponsors. Printed in the United States of America by McNaughton & Gunn, Inc., P.O. Box 10, Ann Arbor, MI 48176. Distributed in the United States by Ubiquity Distributors, 607 Degraw St., Brooklyn, NY 11217. Archive available through JSTOR. Indexed by *Humanities International Complete*. Special thanks to Dara Wier for selecting the 2010 *Mississippi Review* Poetry Series winners.

Contents

One

Two

Three

for Matt

If they cut my bald head open they will find one big boxing glove.

—Marvelous Marvin Hagler

ONE

Photocopy of the Oral Tradition

I haven't papered the osprey's means
of drying out.

To become to bravery
what saying is to the sentence.

Day starts its animals.

We expect
the words will come to us.

The osprey boring in the tall air,
drawn big for its descent,

is hungry for silver.
I copy one

method of ruffling wings,
and the minnow's way of resting.

OTHER PEOPLE'S LIVES

Breathingly, thirty six clouds cross
the hot field. The sky crawls
toward lots. I've never been
so far east of plain and rest
on my back in a slick basement.
As light strands in, a red cockroach
eats a fingerprint (record of
a love affair). Little intervals: angular
cracks in the base of the home
where vines turn flamboyant,
purling from the apothecary garden.
At first, raccoons come singly to the curve
of the fence line. Bent on salt,
they soften to the yard, its block
of shadow growing. New leaf:
I use it to make a drawing in the dirt:
a perfect face with something
the matter. We are not perfect.
An evil, for one, having been in you,
must lay unnamed beside you.
To be clear, we draw exact roundness
from a pint glass, watch raccoons
peel away terrain until nothing
is left at all but gourds. Don't let me go
without telling you my secret:
Death, I tan the blue hides of chills.
Smooth a small living into holdings.

No, Ruin

December, first tile of winter. Yesterday's tracks (concealed

by new snow) activate a pattern in the garden.

Snow gathers in each willful bowl. We eat our weight

until excess reveals itself. That part of *no*

we don't understand: wanting to see what we don't

want to see. I think I remember ruin:

nothing green. Ruin let me discover it when I couldn't wait:

eyes after the rise of proof. Please, just one

more frame before we lose the signal.

The wilderness is banging.

In the Golden Age of Counterfeiting

The beach full of puddles makes the ocean look bigger.
A fish u-turns, wriggles free, or is that
its final display of emphasis? One could search
the beach in vain for signs of finality:
white shells, a wet magazine, the edge of an oar-blade.
I hold the centerfold sideways
until it is taken by the wind. These headlands are shaped
by erosion. Another wave and
another wave pranks the beach. In the chop
float a young boy's corrective shoes, headed out
to where the sun is towed—
the shoes fumbling over the tops of waves,
the radiance flickering inside the current—
that borrowed script of presence & absence
where stage blood or sunlight
fills the hundreds of clear jellyfish splayed along the beach.
Light itself takes a long time.
Language has but one god who made me slow.
What I confess I confess in my echo.

SAFETY BAR

Say nothing rises. A raindrop hits a yellow pencil.
What interests me, drawn as a child would draw it.
Who will explain the unwilling nerves, the black tire-scratch?
Blurred weeds in the blurred ditch. Triangle
of surgery zoned for pills. How shall I
describe these things? Single the deer shuddered
into being. And you only had to say it,
pulling yourself from the wreck
on the wet, green ridge. The bright bumper, the raw
magic of rust dependent on air,
on each huddled atom. Science hasn't heard
the metal speak, nor have we.
Dumb, I find out what evening has to do.
How litter rallies in the wind.
In the welter, I pass an old woman
whistling country. A rebel cell of Hell's
Angels passes me. I shoot my
last whiskey pistol.

PARKS, RECREATION

Except for clearing the land by fire,
not much is legal.

To create tension, debris lay
on one third of an acre.

I'm wrong. This bottle was left here
by kids. They are more

afraid of you than you are of them,
and lay flat as a banner

for soldiers flying over.
We put our blanket down in the fog.

Our kite holds a mirror to nature.
We're dead. Our days are

pressed into slides. I must be coming
down with something—

you are standing right there
in the clearing:

tight white headband, racket
between your thighs.

When I'm wrong, a blush
awakens in the sky.

At the Municipal Pond

As in a lick of yellow reeds,
what we ferry from the mud
is no good to eat. We spread out, stuff
our fingernails with mint. Slowly, sun burns
the forehead largely mute. Longing
returns. A three-day thought held open.
There's no finer hypnosis: a small girl
wades into the pond. The hole she's dug
has a gold fleck in it. I have been trying
to be that gold fleck. Plenty
of game shuttles to the wildflowers
and back. The pond covers up.

Victim Impact Statements

1. 89 degrees under ready-made skies.

2. I've come home, my street is answering yes to Crack.

3. Sick bulbs subdivide our light.

4. We're too close to see it, the muscles of the hungry ones.

5. Ultimately, the smallest puddle depends on luck.

6. The internal reportage is also the external.

7. If what we get in the end is a diorama dropped haphazardly on the sidewalk.

8. From overhead, it is possible to address the whole street.

9. The keynote speaker is a red-shirted kindergartener.

10. Instead of wings, we dream cape.

11. Grass growing through the ribcage of a cat.

12. When I leaned against the smokestacks I heard amniotic fluid.

13. Here comes the dramatic turn.

14. Sweeping back and forth like a stylus.

15. At any moment, the lawnmower will catch up to the grasshopper.

14. To watch the day deepen—I found a camera and am working backwards.

13. The Salvation Army and the YMCA.

12. Across the river, it's already dawn.

11. My arms cross like two thinly lacquered oars.

10. It's too hot to reanimate the landscape.

9. I tuck the plastic sapphire back in my boot.

8. The landlady tight in the neck of a bottle.

7. In black, she was all in black.

6. In the end the street was no Electric Avenue, bless my street.

5. It's punks who fuck with the ATM.

4. Popping blueberries, optimistic.

3. That an El Camino will come.

2. That they will distinguish El Camino.

1. The light turns green. Dramatic!

THE MACULAR DEGENERATION OF MY UNCLE

Look at the bees you don't keep
raiding spring buds.

Bees on the planks, bees
on the legs of summer.

On our decoy dogwoods, empty
cola cans they swarm

in the millions, back from wherever they sleep
in margins made noir

by sunlight on the river. Code
Orange. It was the river

this whole time. The water wide
and blinding. My uncle

ducks. A bee crawls
up his cup. When I look,

a speck of leaf fiber
swims to the corner of one eye.

WHAT MAYS DO

Trees
receive the jolt
of roosting.

The rent was good.

They said it on the radio.
We watched the TV.

Capillaries of the pink cheek.
Flowers in gun barrels.

WHIRL

We fall for distance,
the way we grieve. An end
to this district whose molecules cannot stop spinning
in the downtown air. The dilation
of snow-brittle buildings built only to survive
in outfits of thick ice.

    Each night on the terrace where crows pick locks,
    I paint my little crow gold, and it sings my new favorite
    part and we go for a spin in a good gear

led upward through ceilings we refuse to own,
with the patience of gladioli left all day in elevators.

I am embarrassed,
not for us, but for our building's inability
to translate from its stoop the letters
I drop from the window chased by metallic bugs
blinking like prototypes from the countryside.

    Clean lines hurry wind. All day my window hoards its crust
    of snow. A hawk moth on the Coffee-mate
    folds asleep and out of the cat's dream.

My strategy: all the birds you see in a day.
To cut and paste their matted feathers
into this recurring dream:

    a disproportionate place where the actuality of hunger,
    like a skirt filled with coins,
    like the light in a still life,
    is as pointed now as the steeples we stood below

to study the tongues of bells,
to craft the metalogical laws that govern our listening.

I fall asleep to
the sound of birds bumping glass. I go to bed full
of blackberries and wake as a bride...

Winningly, winter locks itself in a carriage of ice. Outdoors,
zero down. A catalogue trapped in winter branches.

Two

SYNTHETIC

What they took for fine cursive was in fact
dragonflies spawning in the wider distance.
My magnifying glass revealed the wings   ·
on their backs. I got them, I got out of there
we like to imagine. The dragonfly has
teenaged gears, its own blue-lidded eyes.
With winter coming taut as a rink,
I tape it to the window and watch it sleep.
The blue turned to green
turns to white for silver leaves,
red for counterfeit tender.

RECOUNT

My beautiful eyes have just expired. I'll take a fresh ballot
    and that x-ray. It is fall again,

and what the wind does to wings is moderation in the Republic.
    As the parade pinches, we flip

our collars up—each a Roman arch, dove-gray. Soon, night,
    having imbibed already tomb-

fulls of patriarchs, will concede its light to a Tallahassee suburb.

All the banyans are bare of their leaves.

The hornet flies over the Savings and Loan.
The white dog sleeps in the shade.

Yes, the polls have closed.
No, I am not stung. Look me in the iris.

RETURNS

Many days since my last red letter—the stencil a spur, the penny
   sent for vellum. Riding

toward frank need, even mallards leak marrow, honk, and drop
   into the street. Every June,

we rise, histamine-vertiginous, full faces cradling fevers. This year
   was no different: the wait

between flights. I look again at a picture I never liked: me, on a
   trail marked with trash

in the grain of a goodbye, beneath gloom-faced mountains. You,
   washing your ring in the slow-

moving stream (before Ron sung out that he could see
   no bottom).

GLADIOLI PATIENCE

The rigging ran perfectly tethered
to the drapes. Parking one bright thing
against a wall, why is it we can't
be careful? Or urgency is to dumb
as darkness is to doing wrong.
There's a last religion. Put down
the dowsing rods, lured southward like
a tree in a wind that taunts it.
A spider dips itself in cranial light, crawls
all day across the finished room.
Impossible, picturing a white wall,
a terrace where rain pools
in a cactus flower, the rest off
to the Hudson. North American
water where you've already
written *distress, please look.*

Dry-Erase

It takes how many boxes to build a cardboard car?

It's meant to be sad, blue. To suggest something has started and ended.

Beside the YWCA, someone has left:

a ladies' thong sandal, an acetylene torch, a brown swivel chair,

a key change in the weather,

a sudden paper severance—

hear it from my lawyer: ash, the last unit of speech.

Ah, a Styrofoam aviary.

Protest Songs

Every kiss has an army. Deep in the countryside.
    The final campaign is to push your lover over.

That was the ballad as it came to us
    under the honeysuckle, deer watching

through the trees. On the lawn, a late frost
    in which hoofprints circle a rusted barbell.

Do re me my rifle. If you can read this
    we are locked out of the house, waiting

at the door. Attempts to speak the password
    have failed. I have broken my ankle

to make a silence. Dare not say the deepest red leaves
    stick to me. I yawn and you

also yawn. This is, in a way, like war. Long fuses are
    being lit in the city. When you lean

against me an origami crane flowers in my jacket pocket.
    Soon, we'll move on our enemies,

down the list of names. You with your red crest
    and your Roosevelt dime.

LEAN-TO

I.

We clear a breach between trees—
call it what you will. Audubon
says we will chop down the future,
find beauty in militancy.
We will also disappear. The sound
of the campground. The scaffolding
on the riverbank. The oak roots
prowling around for light.

II.

Washington slept here
before crossing the river
with a suitcase full of folios.
Body by moonlight.
A lantern brought low. I'm sorry
for the flash photography. I'm dying
for my country. The holes
in this postcard are for your oars.

III.

A sentence and its syntax lie down together.
One response to fear is arousal.
Which is worth more, the nude
or the memory of the nude?
When I ask the park ranger, he answers
with a question: *Closing your eyes,*
which do you see: the tumor on the back
of the swan, or the arc of an amazing ass?

IV.

A ladybug hits a horse and falls to the ground.
There is a sudden drop in the Dow.
I wrap my hands in double-sided tape
to measure the skull of a snake.
I sit cross-legged on the edge
of a log and smoke.
The enemy plays its last violin.
This whole campground is for sale.

V.

I confess I don't know where the river goes.
Only so far. What is a current?
Wasting its time around my legs
rising. The water is a blank lithograph
hung between two shores.
But still they built.
Go to the window. One more
flood will italicize the trees.

FORENSICS

Blood is not as viscous
as frost

       where I sat for a millennium
    to trouble the surface
    and measure dawn.

Early Roman nature inhabited numina

        until the high peaks
        and well-bored valleys froze.

Today, I tamper with the seal. Take the wool
in my mouth like the halter
before a thaw.

Here are the dozen ways
       winter wants me dead:

1. Knife in a knife storm.
2. Splayed by a barn door.
3. Razor-faced crow.
4. Smoker at the pump.
5. Trouble at the well.
6. Bruised by a billboard.
7. Lose to a bear.
8. Botched metamorphosis.
9. War all over again.
10. I screw off my head.
11. Stone pulling the skull.
12. Can't concentrate.

SAILOR'S KNOT

Say it with the weightiness of a mahogany leg. *Green seas, transparent grave.*
Acknowledge how you hold the boat.
As nautical implications circle the lighthouse, let's don't mistake motive
for motivation (one cloud small, the other swollen).
Some cannot understand. The polarity of earth
directly affects brain waves. Here we are carving
ladies into the woodgrain of a ship.
We come about, hungry, peering down at dying kelp,
doubloons concussed from a coral rut.
Men who take the ocean's oath while balancing on a plank
are seldom heard from again. Their song is looped
with a shifty pitch. Poor and unmoored,
like a fly dispatched. No prospects on deck.
But the tongue is acquainted with the worst.
To tie a mermaid's knot, gather the rope away from you
like an hourglass. Position your hands
around this shape. Letting slip
a love for its denuded body might mean
you'll live a hushed life, your diction dallying.

EAST

A hurricane digs for its salt white dress,
the wilds of which are filled with want. Using its pistons

forms a crude 9. Our place

is like empty drams for it. The hurricane dreams
of logarithms. It is beautiful.

The miles in profile   swing stroked over dress:

One form   most blessed in aft—
no, Eye, because the world is boring.

Recount

A compost heap's genius is you have seen a meditation

if you have looked upon rinds,
the clippings of your own eyes,

the warp of paisley   leaf gassing down like peels.

But you who are
no longer here (hello out there)

your open mile dips
so gracefully   where it would merge

with empty clothes lines   on a Sunday   nice day
and then another.

SNOW INTO RAIN BACK INTO SNOW

A big-rig passes. We are near a border.
Better to speak in signals. In Canada,
to take a powder means to flee full of wine.
Dearest height, dearest weight,
dearest hair color. A detective kneels
near a forest-flung mattress, slitting it open
like a gift. He pretends to wake
in the morning whisper-close, to crawl
across a room, worried perhaps:
the fact that we are here, that you are not.
Your yellow skin becomes highway
and circuitry. A geographic
of routes branching into ever more
distant branches, leading back to the world's
first auroral fuse, now burnt out.
Only the bark paintings of the Songish
tribes prove it was ever here,
that there had been a great battle,
a criminal comet, a motionless storm.

GRAVELLY HILL

Arrangements arrive and we rearrange
flowers contrapuntally. I go downstairs

and outside where the pigeons are
uneager to alight. Beyond the train tracks,

a register. We had come out, we had recognized
an absence, tracking it by what it costs.

July, and the station gives pastel tickets.
The afterimage of each passing train

contains its giant bolts and its long shadow.
On the gravelly hill, ditchreeds fan the air

but do not fall. Over the train tracks
hover dragonflies, stone cairns

where weeds thrive, some sideways. Almost
everything has occurred. A contest

between two seasons: the green fabric and
the bright bedclothes. A schedule

stenciled on a single cell, a timepiece left
on the bathroom sink where someone,

reaching through a beaded chain,
has touched the brown spots of summer.

And you think you saw this:
how contingency and collapse rekindle.

Outside, a few waiting faces study the tops
of branches, the displaced smoke:

a soldier on the platform wields cologne.
The memorial benches harden and jut.

A girl scout shrieks, lifting her skirt.
A squirrel flips a wood chip and freezes.

THREE

THESE DUTCH DOORS

A leaf grows twin identities

                         (as if hearted)

Silence falls on the lawn

                         (for all who fell)

The leaf is in my pocket

                         (would daze, bewilder)

Why we wear gloves

                         (hoisting a flag)

So that I fist the air

                         (words worth repeating)

A leaf falls, incomplete

                         (a sudden place)

Hands over eyes

                         (I am dressed now).

OF EXHAUSTION

While out hunting, Mao declares sparrows
enemies of the state,

                                  hyphenating flight.

Out of my window I see a thousand Mosin rifles,
smell tea
       and hanging ruined rugs.

                               Sparrows,
                               tracing funnels of sky,
                               start as we do:

salute our satellites,
rehearse again
and again a vaulting.

*

Mao steps into a stubbled field.
                               Linen flags
                               marking the acre.
                  His scent
                  is pressed earth,
                  the leaves
                  of wet books.

Our man on the inside
takes an aspirin.

                               A silo
                               teeters. Almost no one
                               goes in there.

For days, men prevent sparrows
from landing.

Sing: *how they do muffle the rain.*

What if Marvelous Marvin Hagler:

Feathered the severe weapon laid at his feet.

Danced some.
Saw the dark part heal.

Was worse.

Reverb.

Divorce.

Was mocking bird verse.

Reverse.

Toast.

Curled his hand around

more
than air.

Left our fields in peace.

Was here.
His pepper.

Let us wear roller skates.

Delaware

When the generals finally head to the showers, they're beginning to peel.
Nodding off like trees and sleeping through the slide show.

A pack of more than four is referred to as a "slap" of generals.
Tongues dryer than attic beams.

"I love you," spoken by a general, contains more shelves than a mausoleum.
We wake, we find a mirror for the crack of the door.

Reshuffle "generals" to spell "earn," and it also kicks out its "legs."
Approaching the ridge at Bulls Island, we are raw.

When the generals ride in from the field, they do so out of shyness.
Whoever is sacked must leave the inn at dawn.

"The Generals," sung allegretto, sounds like acorns hitting wrought iron.
Picture an actress composed to take a blow.

In the last days of a campaign, one rim-shot stops a horse fight.
At times we are acting, and at others, more real.

Calling forth whoever will give his breast to the bullets of a mob.
In one slide, a pamphleteer describes a lost pet.

I believe there is something else entirely to the generals, but I will not leave you.
In the snow, acres of corn slap shut their husks.

A nervous waitress bounces a Hessian baby on her knee.
A general leans into a keyhole clogged with hammers.

From the opposite bank of the river, a watchmaker signals with his hat.
As it breaks the skin, the bullet calls out to the bobwhite.

We approach neither from the North nor South, East nor West.
The touch that follows will not mean "truce."

A general leans against a streetlamp, flipping a foreign coin.
A bell rings and holds. To cross one's self and the river.

First Person Omniscient

I climb a ladder by preoperative light.
In the gutter, some obstruction:
characters round or flat, corseted or not.

Nothing bent architecturally
but the center bolt. I climb to where
the mechanism fails, where the gutter

bows each year in one direction.
Holes here, some rot. An obvious
point of disrepair. The paint is from

another time. Pieces come off
in my hands, dusting my thighs. Reverie
opens its little window in the real

November. I scoot into place
horizontally. Then, tracers of rain.
Written in mud, a treatise on exes.

[ONLY BIRDS CHEER UP]

Only birds cheer up
         the dry canal
         echoing back Verdi

         from the flower constructed sirens
            of borough air radio
as day samples

         you with a bow
         among the weeds.

Homesickness

A lake with your first name. Along a hollowed-out hill. You'll
    take it as a sign.
Into the anatomy of bells. Walk it into a ring of stones. Drag it
    through a South Jersey town
whose blank marquees predict a neutral eternity.
All "what-ifs" suffer as technology lags. For instance, the mouth
has a weather; no one notices the red phone inside it,
colors and things halved we want to have sex with.
Children see an obelisk flowering into the stars.
Children bouncing on a bundle of moss. Awaiting the day they
    can smoke
out night windows with a view
of the last great campfire, redolent with the burning of letters.
Until the day we say anything will do.
Kisses and information.
Try lipstick and the lake will confess.
Like an August with laws.

PTERODACTYL

Tiny are the tugboats crisscrossing the sound

with what may well be arms.

No longer playthings unalloyed,

we are the world again

deciphering one another's code in the campground dusk,

storming a small, bay-stained beach

where all seesaws reach a comfortable pause

and all digging will be archaeology,

given the mammalian bays and lovers swimming

in and out of tributaries

beneath the bridge of your long johns where it's raining again

and you pucker, what we were born to do,

or feel up little fish. I was going to

wade in, but the difference between your bait and mine

is a free-spinning skirt,

as detonated day doubles back with variable speed—

isn't the power house transitive,

and any song, el tempo adagio, worth singing?

Always you will get high,

but the moon will rise over you

and the tent and the guns.

As You Cradle the New Bow in Your Arms

Horizon is human:
far fades there.

You make a flat pebble
skip across the water.

And if at the end
of journeying

there's no weather?
You burn your arrows for heat.

Sing
the bliss of the made

heat you thought
promised nothing.

The Rocket Hour

Half-forgotten Nike rocket in a recession,
radar obsessed.

        Our pupils fall open
        matter of factly,
        the sky smoldering like a quilt.

Rocket faces basics:
        To find its way
        without eyes.

            This is when everything begins:

        I play   hide
        and seek
            with the rocket.
And when I say I
it only makes the floor slick.

So I'll leave slowly counting down from ten.

        Without coordinates,
        leaving meant

            marching home
            alone,
            a stillborn hawk
            in my vest.

We master selective forgetting.

The rocket,

a white coasting kiln

powered up by beautiful talk,
flies over us

and perms our hair.

Dear rocket,
(in a silent script)

*Loss as law
brings no surprise.
The vows of the wounded
don't cohere.*

On TV,
a bugle cries
at the edge of an embassy.

One at dawn.

BURYING A ST. JOSEPH IN THE BACKYARD

He has never been called loser, he is digging a hole.
The sun throws in its voice. Cirrus clouds
he must be mostly absent to see. If he prays
for a higher offer, the words are unknown to anyone,
like a room that is empty and dark. There,
he watches his own shadow, with all its weight,
packing curtains in a hard-shell case.
Summer is going and taking with it every clear idea
the windows ever had. Nights: a net of mosquitoes
in a capital hangs dusklit on each light.
Dew uncurls the fists of dry leaves along the patio.
He holds. As now his dogs dig up the textured clay
and bring it in the house. He clears a space
nowhere in particular. For a moment,
there isn't a Weehawken. Around his head,
bubble wrap. He is breaking it and breathing in.

Minor Emergency

I. BROADCAST [FROM THE PLACES WE FLED]

Heard the mannequins creak
as the sun tanked. In the busy parlor
where paintings were hung
and now melt into decanters, the indefinite
ratchets back. The wind blows off
a shingle or two.
Behind the parlor, the water tower makes a shadow
like a bridesmaid inflated
to twice her normal size.
At day's end we don't ask.
We walk to where we'll never be heard.
The natural history of distance
gets loud in the trees.
Then nothing. Somewhere else
a wedding and a war.
I heard them speaking
in the other room, in this weird light,
about our right to hide.
"A took tulip never opens."
This, written on my cast.

II. A STATE OF GRACE

Brut, brut champagne. I only get five minutes in this suit. The time it takes to compare lives. No, not the shyness. The drone. Patterns like tractor tracks, gorgeous trees, young flowers between my teeth. My throat is sore with the world's question. We stupefy magnitude with meaning. Nightfall. Fallen night. The cellist errs, misplacing the final notes of the nocturne. And I was almost completed.

III. EMERGEN-C

Because the boy is not ours

with the ghost-like face

he will pay

the bill at the end of the world

with a name he stole,

lamb it

to local sales events,

come crunching through the snow

with a wreath for each door

and still not feel.

IV. EXIT [IF THE BLIND NEED NUDGING]

The whole city is cross. The cuffs of its jacket still taste of tornado. Over the hilltops, our toys tiptoe back to the factory. Earlier I said I find comfort in gossip. But nothing happens here beyond rite and riddance. The dog takes the leash in his mouth. A bottle rocket lay in the snow. A canary lay in the snow. I dreamt my father, uncle, brother were throwing pies at a bear. But there's no pie in the ivy. No snowball in the sentence. No teeth coming down. If only as a wake, I sometimes say day and mean delay.

American Funeral

Weight I gain
gambols
above leather.
Leaned against it,
you, like
before the bulb
gave light
to mise en scène,
to anything
from the parlor drape.
Work, I could stay
awake for days,
word up
in my mouth,
moon over
the Credit Union
all alone.

EMPIRE

They lie on their backs for calisthenics.
From the air or the belfries, each body a minus sign.

That's my last duchess growing into movement.
Tied to her bodice, twenty balloons.

This moment some mornings everything's possible.
The grass is full of shoes. All are collected

and checked for obscenity. Each one,
a possible beginning. This season, we have angled

toward the ether. Some bit down on death,
pulling stunts like clouds pull a tower.

We pray, though only as a protective thing.
In the chapel, an abutment: stone

upon stone. Here, something tall in a terrific glare
sways to unlistened-to music. The gallows

give up their depths. The cocoons
are shot through with gravel. The cabbage rose

in the sun garden is orphaned to the bees.
Who booked such dark birds to discover us?

Or

Two crayons float toward a leaf.
Chlorine revises them.

You set adrift in post-op sleep.
If we could just

return to the tilt
of May. Inside, I am

tagging Ghost on this mirror.
If you know,

what use is the thought
after this one?

About the Author

Christopher Salerno is from New Jersey. His poems have appeared in several journals, including *Colorado Review, Denver Quarterly, Boston Review, Jubilat, American Letters and Commentary, LIT,* and others. His first book, *Whirligig* was published by Spuyten Duyvil Publishing House and featured by Barnes & Noble. He teaches in the English Department at North Carolina State University and is co-curator of The So and So Series.